HARRIET BEECHER STOWE:
Woman Crusader
An American Pioneer Biography

Harriet Beecher Stowe saw how inhuman slavery was and set out to do something about it. She wrote a novel, *Uncle Tom's Cabin,* that was one of the most popular books ever published. It made people in the North angry at slavery and people in the South angry at Harriet. Abraham Lincoln called her the little woman who started the big Civil War.

As author Jean Rouverol shows in this moving biography, Harriet was born poor and suffered great personal sorrows. But she overcame her troubles and became the first famous American woman author.

HARRIET BEECHER STOWE:
Woman Crusader

By Jean Rouverol   *Illustrated by Charles Brey*

AN AMERICAN ♣ PIONEER BIOGRAPHY

G. P. PUTNAM'S SONS,   NEW YORK

CONTENTS

1. THE BEECHERS

There were eight vigorous, noisy, argumentative, and highly intelligent Beecher children. The oldest was Catherine, sixteen, and the youngest was the baby, Charles. They lived in a big old house in Litchfield, Connecticut, that looked over the countryside toward Prospect Hill.

Five-year-old Harriet, or Hattie, as everyone called her, was the sixth Beecher if you started at the top and worked down. She often stood in the doorway and watched the beautiful sunsets. Long before she could put her feelings

7

into words, those views from the front doorway filled her with awe and wonder.

Her father was the pastor of the Litchfield Congregational Church at that time — 1816. He preached thunderous sermons about hellfire that made one's skin tingle and sent shivers up the spine. But the Reverend Lyman Beecher was not nearly as terrifying at home as in the pulpit. He played with his children and taught them music so there could be family concerts around the stove after dinner. Sometimes he even took off his shoes and danced the hornpipe, though the children's mother objected because it wore out his socks. He made great boisterous games of cutting wood with his boys. As a reward, he would take them on all-day fishing trips to Great Pond.

The three Beecher girls weren't included on those trips. They had to study or do chores around the house until Pa and the boys came trooping back in the evening, joyous and exhausted, to clean and cook their day's catch of fish. Hattie envied her brothers those glorious days.

When Hattie had been younger, her mother, Roxana, used to read aloud to the children in the evening. But lately she had been ill and spent her days in bed. So Catherine took over the reading. Sometimes the older children told the younger ones tales of Beechers in the past. The first Beecher to come to America had arrived just seventeen years after the *Mayflower*. There was a long line of well-read, highly respected blacksmith Beechers — all the way down to Uncle Lot, who had tried to teach Pa to be a farmer. When Uncle Lot saw the first furrow young Lyman plowed, he decided that Lyman should go to college and become a minister — because he certainly would never make a farmer.

Then there was the story of Aunt Mary Foote Hubbard, who had died three years ago. Or *was* it just a story? Hattie thought she could remember a lady with a pale, sad face and a cough like Mother's cough now. She had come all the way from the West Indies, where her husband was a planter. Her husband kept slaves, whom Aunt Mary had seen cruelly treated. She said that she "wished the island might sink into the ocean, with all its sin and misery, and that I might sink with it." Hattie could recall the words so clearly that she was almost sure she remembered Aunt Mary saying them.

Hattie, who had been born on June 14, 1811, in Litchfield, was quieter than most of her brothers and sisters. She was quick-witted and liked to make her family laugh. But often she was lost in thought, moving in a kind of daze. Her brothers would say then that she was "owling about." She had a remarkable memory and learned to read when very young. Once, after she had pitched in with the boys on a wood-cutting spree, she heard her father say, "Wisht Hattie'd been a boy; she'd do more work than any of 'em!" Though she knew she could never grow up to hammer an anvil like her great-

grandfathers or be a preacher like Pa, she longed to do something to make her family proud of her.

Later, people who knew the Beechers would say that two things made them different from anyone else: a sense of mission — and a sense of humor.

That sense of mission would one day make Harriet famous. She was to become the first widely known American woman writer — and thus be a pioneer to other girls and women who wished to write. One of her books, *Uncle Tom's Cabin,* would indeed affect the course of United States history.

But all this was far in the future for little Harriet Beecher of Litchfield.

In the year her mother, Roxana, was ill, the family was even poorer than usual. Perhaps this worry had caused Roxana's health to break. In any event, the children were allowed less time with the pale, serene woman who sat propped up in bed, growing weaker every day.

And Pa stopped romping with the children; he was silent and worried.

One September night Hattie, asleep in the little nursery under the eaves which she shared with her two younger brothers, Henry Ward and Charlie, dreamed that Mother was well again. The dream seemed so real that she started up joyously in bed — to find that someone had come into the darkened room to tell her that Mother had died.

Poor father! His duty as minister had been to ease the fears of the dying and to comfort the families left behind, assuring them that heaven was a happier place than earth. His strong faith had comforted so many people, but now it could not help him. He was like a man lost. He could not write a sermon. When he tried to give a mealtime blessing, he wept and could not say anything.

Each Beecher child tried in his own way to keep Mother alive in his heart. One day Catherine and Hattie found three-year-old Henry

Ward out in the garden digging, his face flushed and his fair curls damp with perspiration. When Catherine asked him what he was doing, he said, "I'm digging down to find Mamma."

Soon Father sent Hattie to visit Nutplains, in Guilford, where Grandmother Foote lived. After a long carriage ride, Hattie was carried into a white farmhouse where a lovely white-haired old lady sat before a fire. Hattie was lifted into her lap and wrapped in loving arms while tears rolled down the old lady's face and wet Hattie's own. This was her mother's mother, and this was the house where Roxana had grown up and met Father.

She learned that Roxana was the grand-daughter of a general in the Revolutionary War. She had given up her Episcopalian religion because Father insisted she share his faith. Hattie heard stories of Roxana's goodness and quiet strength from everyone who had known her. Surrounded by loving memories of her mother, Hattie began to feel comforted.

2. GROWING UP

Pa was determined that all his boys should enter the ministry. Poor as they were, he made sure they went to the best colleges in New England. He also wanted his girls to have well-trained minds. Thus, as soon as each Beecher girl was old enough, she was sent to Miss Pierce's Female Academy in Litchfield.

While Hattie was still too young for school, she prowled about the big Beecher house looking for something to read. For want of anything else, she tried reading her father's old sermons or those of the Puritan preacher Jonathan Edwards. Far more exciting than sermons were the poems of Lord Byron. Her Aunt Esther, who had come to help take care of the Beecher children, introduced her to them. Hattie didn't understand them very well, but she loved the sound of the poems.

Her happiest hours were spent in the attic. In order to get there, she had to pass a little chamber high up in the chimney, which Pa used for smoking meats. The first time she opened the little door in the brick wall, she peered into a fearsome place of smoke and flames. It looked so much like a glimpse of hell described in the book *Pilgrim's Progress,* by John Bunyan, that she ran away in fright.

The attic itself was shadowy and sweet-smelling, with bundles of dried herbs, piles of pumpkins and quinces, bins of corn and oats. There were also colonies of mice and rats, which the Beecher cats simply ignored. It was there that Hattie, delving down into barrels of old papers and sermons, discovered books. She found a dog-eared copy of the *Arabian Nights* and sat down to read it from cover to cover.

Still deeper in the barrel was a book, called *Magnalia,* written by a Puritan preacher named Cotton Mather. It told of witches, Indians, and the Pilgrim Fathers settling in New England. It made her feel that the Pilgrims had made this land sacred in their search for religious freedom.

On July 4 the Beecher family went to the Independence Day celebrations in Litchfield. There Colonel Tallmadge, who had been an officer in George Washington's Army, read aloud the Declaration of Independence. Hattie, listening to its thrilling words, longed — as she had when she read *Magnalia* — to *do* something. She didn't know quite what it was — to fight or to make some statement in her own words that would help the cause of freedom in America. Yet what could a young girl do?

One stormy night, while her father was away

on a trip, Hattie was awakened by a commotion and sat up in bed. She heard a familiar, hearty laugh from the doorway. "Why, here's Pa!" she cried.

Then a pleasant voice called out behind him, "And here's Ma!"

Hattie saw a woman with beautiful reddish-brown hair and bright blue eyes. Her name was Harriet Porter, and her home was Portland, Maine. She kissed the upturned faces of Hattie and her two little brothers, then told them she loved children and would be their new mother. They wanted to get up, but she promised them she would still be there when they woke up in the morning.

And she was.

When Hattie was eight years old, she entered Miss Pierce's Female Academy in Litchfield. Her favorite instructor taught English composition. Young Hattie, supposedly busy with her own work, sat at her desk enthralled by his lectures to the older students. Eventually she got up courage to write him an essay on the most difficult subject she could think of: The Difference Between the Natural and the Moral Sublime. Though more than half her words were misspelled, the teacher did not laugh; instead, he gently encouraged her.

A few years later, when Hattie had written many essays and her spelling had improved, one of her compositions was read aloud at a school exhibition. Though the composition did not bear her name, Hattie noticed that her father listened with interest. Then he asked a teacher, "Who wrote that?"

"Your daughter, sir!"

It was the proudest moment of Hattie's life thus far.

3. THE USE OF TALENTS

Hattie's sister Catherine, engaged to a brilliant young mathematician, suffered a cruel blow when her fiancé was drowned on his way to study in Europe. Catherine, heartbroken, decided to devote the rest of her life to doing some good. Sooner or later all the Beechers arrived at that decision. Catherine looked about her for a cause which seemed to need her and thought she found it in women's education.

Thus, in 1823, Catherine Beecher and her sister Mary opened a school for young ladies

in Hartford, Connecticut. Hattie went there as a student the next year. Before she was fifteen, she was teaching there, too.

In her teens Hattie was small, slender, and serious. When her thoughts were turned inward and she was "owling about," nobody would have thought her pretty. But when she was happy and animated, her eyes sparkled, and her friends would be suddenly astonished to find that Hattie was so beautiful.

She had already decided that she wanted to be a famous writer and earn enough money to build a beautiful, big house. She had even found the spot — amid a grove of oaks on a small stream near Hartford. And she made close friends at school, the first she had ever known. She should have been happy. Then why wasn't she?

She was worried about her character! In quiet moments in her room or when wandering about the countryside, she fretted about her soul. Her father's stern religion had taught her that man was sinful, that he was damned from birth. But Hattie couldn't feel damned or sinful. Midway between childhood and womanhood, she was acutely aware of the loveliness of the world about her — birds, fresh dewy mornings, sunlight. How could her father's God of wrath have given such beautiful things to people who were damned? Hattie couldn't make sense of it and decided there must be something wrong with her. Sometimes, despairing, she wished she could die young.

At other times the Beecher sense of mission caught up with her, and she wrote to her family, "God has given me talents, and I will lay them at His feet...."

At home, Lyman Beecher had decided that a man with eleven children (for by now his young wife had given him three more) could no longer live on a salary of $800 a year and firewood. So he was ready to leave Litchfield when he received a call from the Hanover Street Church in Boston. There, with his fire-breathing sermons against dueling, drunkenness, Catholics, Unitarians, and husbands who weren't true to their wives, he became known as the most prominent, popular, and powerful preacher in America. Soon he was urged to go to Cincinnati, Ohio, and become the first president of a new school for clergymen—Lane Theological Seminary.

This delighted Catherine, who felt that the raw new frontier states needed her teaching talents. And so in 1832 twenty-one-year-old Harriet found herself traveling west with her enormous family to begin a new life.

As they bounced along the roads in a chartered stagecoach, the Beechers laughed, argued about philosophy, and sang—never dreaming that events would occur in the Midwest which would commit them passionately to one side in a terrible conflict. And in this great drama to come, every Beecher would play his part—but the largest part would be Harriet's.

Cincinnati, Ohio, in the 1830's was a bustling river town. The broad Ohio River passed the

town on its way to the great Mississippi. Slave-owning was forbidden in Ohio. But across the river in Kentucky slaveowning was legal.

Posted on fences, walls, and barns in Cincinnati were advertisements offering rewards for the capture of slaves who had escaped across the river from their masters in Kentucky. Every now and then a steamboat of slaves, chained to one another, passed the Cincinnati waterfront. Even in Ohio and the North there were few people who questioned whether slavery was right or wrong. Scarcely anyone worried about the Negro families that must have been wrenched apart when a boatload of slaves started their journey.

The Beechers thought that slavery was unchristian. But, they reasoned, plantation owners had invested many hundreds of dollars in their slaves. It would not be fair to deprive them of their property by abolishing slavery outright. At any rate, the Beechers were so caught up in the excitement of new careers and a new household that they were hardly aware of the human tragedies taking place almost under their eyes. The Reverend Beecher was busy with his new school and also was the pastor of a Presbyterian church in town. Catherine's Western Female Academy was opening. Harriet was excited over the publication of her first book — a children's geography, written over Catherine's name.

Harriet also joined a literary group, the Semicolon Club, whose members met to read their writings aloud. There she made friends with pretty Eliza Stowe, whose plump, balding young husband, Calvin, taught Bible history at Father's new college. Another member was the editor of *Western* magazine. It was an exciting day for Harriet when he awarded her a $50 prize for her first published story – a description of Uncle Lot, who had tried so hard to make a farmer of Father. The prize gave Harriet her first confidence in herself as a writer.

So she made a busy, useful life for herself. She had no suitors, perhaps because she was so shy. And thus far she had not yet discovered her mission. Toward the end of her third year in Ohio, however, she found a suitor.

Pretty Eliza Stowe had died during one of the city's hot, cholera-ridden summers. Her husband, Calvin, was desolate. Harriet tried to comfort him, and somehow what began as sympathy turned into love. In January, 1836, they were married. In December twin girls were born to them, and Harriet's tranquil years had ended.

4. SHADOWS OF SLAVERY

Arguments for and against slavery gradually began to concern the Beechers. Lyman Beecher had often said that the people opposed to slavery — called abolitionists — were like men who would burn down the house to get rid of the rats. But during the first year of Harriet's marriage, something happened in Cincinnati that roused everyone's emotions.

A man in Alabama named James Birney, deeply moved by an abolitionist preacher, had freed all his slaves and moved to Cincinnati. There he began to publish a paper urging the immediate abolition of slavery. Soon an unruly mob broke into his office and threatened to destroy his printing press. Then a group of "respectable" men decided that Birney should be run out of town. Harriet was outraged. She and her brother Henry Ward — who at that time was editing a small newspaper of his own with Harriet's help — printed the story. Every other paper in town either ignored it or favored the mob.

Tempers ran high. One evening Harriet discovered her affectionate, easygoing brother Henry Ward in the family kitchen melting down lead into bullets. "What are you making those for?" she asked.

"To kill men with, Hattie!" he replied.

Birney courageously refused to leave Cincinnati. That night the mob broke into his office once more, wrecked the printing press, and threw it into the river. Then the mob went on to tear down houses of law-abiding Negro residents. They rampaged on, growing more destructive until even some proslavery citizens were disgusted. At last the mob "slunk into their dens, and were still," Harriet wrote. "That summer and fall," she said later, "opened my eyes to the real nature of slavery as they had never been opened before."

She felt a great urge to do something. But what could she do? She still felt the abolitionists were too extreme. Yet there seemed no in-between position she could take. And the violence of the proslavery men was forcing her and all humane people closer to the abolitionist point of view.

The following year her older brother Edward had a similar experience — but with more tragic results.

Edward was then head of Illinois College. His friend Elijah Lovejoy had been printing articles against slavery in his paper the *Observer* in St. Louis. But feeling it was too dangerous there, he moved his printing press to Alton, Illinois. Edward helped Lovejoy unload the press from the

riverboat and store it in a warehouse. Then, after he had gone home, mobs attacked the warehouse and killed Lovejoy. If Edward had remained with his friend, he certainly would have been killed, too.

Even the Reverend Beecher's church was split between those for and those against slavery. While Lyman Beecher and his sons were at a church convention in Philadelphia, terrible violence broke out there. Mobs set fire to Abolition Hall, and firemen refused to try to put out the blaze. Then African Hall was set afire, and mobs cut the fire hoses. Hattie heard about all these shameful events and remembered them.

She heard many stories about the desperate measures slaves took to escape from cruel masters or to avoid being sold downriver or away from their families. Sometimes a slave in Kentucky managed to escape his pursuers by crossing the Ohio River just before the ice broke up, jumping from ice floe to ice floe until he reached the northern bank.

One day the problem arose in Harriet's own household.

She had working for her a young part-Negro woman with a charming, bright little boy. Harriet had hired her supposing that she had been freed by her former owners. One day, however, Calvin heard that the young woman was actually a runaway slave and that her former master was in town looking for her. The young woman begged for help. That night, with a storm raging, Calvin Stowe and Charles Beecher bundled her and her child into a carriage and took them over dark, muddy country roads to the farmhouse of a man named Van Zandt, who was, they knew, a member of the underground railway. This meant that his house was a hiding place for escaped slaves on their way to freedom in the North or Canada.

The big farmer came out to meet their carriage, shielding his candle with his hand. Calvin called to him, "Are you the man who will shelter a poor woman and her child from slave catchers?"

"I rather think I am," answered Van Zandt. He took in the two refugees and kept them safe till he could send them on their way to the next stop on the underground railway.

Harriet never forgot these events.

At home her life was often hard. Calvin, rich in ancient languages, was rich in nothing else. Often the Stowes could not make ends meet. Harriet had one baby after another. Sometimes the poverty and confusion were so great that Harriet became ill.

But her sister Catherine and several of Harriet's friends were convinced that her hobby of writing could help the Stowes.

They made neat copies of some of her sketches and sent them off to magazines. Harriet was amazed when she received a check from one of the magazines. She used it to buy a feather bed and pillows. After that, whenever the Stowes

needed something or found themselves in debt, she would try to find a few hours in which to sit down and write another story.

It was not easy. She had to snatch chance moments, sitting in the nursery with children tumbling about her feet or in the kitchen while bread was baking. Harriet often thought it was like "rowing against wind and tide." There was always a baby teething or a new helper in the kitchen to be taught to bake bread or pumpkin pie. When she mislaid her inkstand, she found it on top of the teakettle. Her papers were on a table in the midst of flour, rolling pin, and lard. Even at the end of the day she did not rest but read aloud to her older children — especially the books of Sir Walter Scott, which she herself had loved when young.

Even in her weariest moments Harriet believed that some important work would one day be put into her hands.

Loving, understanding Calvin gave her every encouragement, telling her that by her writing she had "the power to form the mind of the West." When her health broke down again after the birth of her sixth child, she went to a health resort in Vermont to recover. Calvin wrote her there, "The fact is, I cannot live without you.... There is no woman like you in this wide world. Who else has so much talent with so little self-conceit? ... So much literature with so little nonsense? ... So much sweetness with so little softness...."

Harriet replied: "If you were not my dearly beloved husband, I should certainly fall in love with you."

When Harriet came home, Calvin became ill and had to take his turn at the Vermont health resort, leaving Harriet overwhelmed by work and debts.

Then cholera again struck Cincinnati.

The deaths rose to 120 a day; some fell dead in the streets. Two of Harriet's children caught the disease. Henry, the oldest boy, recovered. But the baby, Charles, died.

Later Harriet wrote, "It was my only prayer to God that such anguish might not be suffered in vain....I felt I could never be consoled for it, unless this crushing of my heart *might enable me to work out some great good to others.*"

5. A GROWING FAMILY

At last Harriet was leaving Cincinnati.

Most of her family had already returned to the East and were active in the campaign against slavery. Her brother Edward was in Boston, preaching abolitionist sermons; his house was a way station on the underground railway. And Henry Ward had long been an antislavery preacher in Brooklyn, New York, where he brought slaves to his pulpit and persuaded his congregation to buy their freedom.

But the government in Washington did not share the Beechers' beliefs. The Fugitive Slave Act had just been passed. This meant that it was now a federal crime to shelter a runaway slave, even in free territory. Freed Negroes were given no chance to prove they were free; they would not be allowed jury trial, but the simple word of any white man would be taken as proof that they were slaves.

All the Beechers were outraged at the new law. Even Harriet's mild younger brother Charles, then a minister in New Jersey, preached a sermon on "the duty of disobedience to wicked laws."

Harriet had her hands full, getting her family settled in a pleasant old house in Brunswick, Maine, where Calvin had been appointed to the faculty of Bowdoin College. At first she did not participate in the Beecher protests. She made curtains, struggled with a kitchen sink that had no water, and had a new baby — another boy named Charles. In the midst of all the household turmoil she received a letter from Edward Beecher's wife describing heartbreaking scenes in Boston since the new law had gone into effect. There had been wholesale roundups of former slaves, who until recently had found refuge in Boston. Negro families had been cruelly separated.

Harriet read the letter aloud to her children to its final words: "Hattie, if I could use the pen as you can, I would write something that would make this whole nation feel what an accursed thing slavery is!"

Then she crumpled the letter in a fist. "God helping me, I will write something!" she vowed. "I *will if I live!*"

But one more seed was to be planted before she was ready to write.

Early in 1851 she visited her brother Edward and his wife in Boston where she met a Negro minister, Josiah Henson. This gentle clergyman was a former slave. He described seeing his father bloodied and helpless on the ground after a savage beating by a white overseer — for the "crime" of defending his wife. He told Harriet of beatings he had received and of his escape to freedom. Yet he showed no bitterness toward his persecutors. Harriet, always deeply religious, saw in this man something she could only describe as Christ-like. And the mental image of the beaten Negro father haunted her.

Not long afterward there was a communion service in her church in Brunswick. Harriet sat in her pew with her children, listening to the sermon. She fell into one of her reveries. Did the preacher quote Jesus' words, or did Harriet hear them only in her mind? — "Inasmuch as ye have done it unto one of the least of my brethren, ye have done it unto me." Suddenly she imagined she saw a Negro dying from the lashes of a slave whip. His name would be Uncle Tom. She fancied she saw two Negro overseers, made brutal by their villainous white master, becoming awed and ashamed by the gentle forgiveness of the dying man.

The story unfolded in pictures before her eyes; she could hardly keep from weeping. When the service ended, she went home quickly, locked

herself in her room, and began to write what she had imagined. Later she said that she felt as though a great wind were blowing through her mind.

When she ran out of writing paper, she finished the story on heavy wrapping paper.

That evening when her children were clustered around her after supper, she read them what she had written. When she finished, she found the two oldest boys in tears. "Oh, Mamma," sobbed eleven-year-old Freddie, "slavery is the cruelest thing in the world!"

But there were many household problems and little time. Harriet put the scraps of paper away and forgot them.

A few weeks later she discovered Calvin reading them, tears pouring down his cheeks. He had come upon the bits of paper in a drawer. It was more than a story, he told her. It must be the climax of a book about slavery, and she must write it at once.

At last Harriet had found her mission.

Now the stories of slaves and slavery she had heard in Cincinnati came rushing back to her. As the book began to take shape, she remembered a visit she and a friend had made to a Kentucky plantation. This became the Shelby plantation in the first chapter of her story. She remembered a little Negro girl she had taught in Sunday school — a child brought to Ohio when her owners moved there and freed. Harriet recalled the laughing face, the lighthearted voice saying, "I 'spect I just growed. Nobody made me." In Harriet's pages this little girl became the character named Topsy.

And Simon Legree, the hateful, slave-beating villain of the book? Harriet's brother Charles had met such a man more than ten years before on a Mississippi riverboat. Charles had told Hattie years before of the brutal plantation owner who boasted that his knuckles had become tough as hickory from knocking down slaves.

Harriet wrote on. Many of her experiences took their places on those pages. Early in the book a ten-month-old baby was sold away from his mother. Harriet wrote, "But the woman did not scream. The shot had passed too straight and direct through the heart for cry or tear." She had never lost a baby to a slave trader — but her grief at the loss of baby Charley to cholera was as fresh as the day it had happened. She had only to let herself remember sitting by Charley's crib, watching his suffering and knowing there was nothing in the world she could do to save him.

The editor of an abolitionist magazine offered her $300 for the story. It seemed like a lot of money, for at the time both he and Harriet thought it would be a three-part serial. But months later the story was still unfolding. Subscribers to the *National Era* were waiting breathlessly for the next installment — and the next.

The story was still running in the magazine when the John P. Jewett Company agreed to publish it as a novel, even though they didn't think many people would buy a book about slavery. As Harriet's chapters kept arriving, they wrote her a protest: Couldn't she make it shorter?

Harriet wrote back that she wasn't making up the story; it was making itself up, and she couldn't stop until it was done.

At last Harriet's outpouring of emotion wore itself out, and the story drew to a close. Harriet bundled the pages together and sent them off to the publisher. Years before she had wanted to earn enough to build a beautiful, big house. Her wishes were more modest now; she hoped only that this book would sell enough copies to buy her a silk dress.

On March 20, 1852, *Uncle Tom's Cabin* appeared on the bookstands of America.

6. SUDDEN FAME

Almost immediately every copy of the first edition was sold. The publisher printed another edition — then another. Harriet could scarcely believe what was happening. Before long the demand for *Uncle Tom's Cabin* became so great that eight power printing presses, running day and night, could not keep up with it.

Best of all, the publisher wrote Harriet that people in the South were buying the book as fast as people in the North. Harriet had hoped, as she wrote of the sufferings of Negroes in bondage, that slaveowners would realize the tragedies they were causing and would be moved to free their slaves. She had tried hard to show both the good and the bad sides of the system and had portrayed two of her three slaveowners as kindly, humane men. As for Simon Legree, the book's villain, she had been careful to write that he had come originally from New England. The abolitionists might not like it, she thought, but the Southerners would.

One of her friends in the South wrote that it would be the great peacemaker. "It will unite North and South," wrote her friend.

But suddenly readers and critics realized the book was more than a moving human story. It was a battle cry against slavery. The abolitionists began to hail the book. And Southerners turned on it and began to denounce it furiously, whether they had read it or not. Letters filled with such hatred and venom that she could hardly read them began to reach Harriet. One day a package containing *a black human ear* came in the mail.

Now it became impossible to buy a copy of the book in the South, where booksellers were afraid to sell it. Anyone circulating a copy ran the risk of being run out of town. And to Hattie's astonishment, a religious paper in New York accused her of being antichristian.

Apart from the South, the book was selling more copies than anything else in print except the Bible. Within the first year 300,000 copies had been sold in the United States alone. And in England and the British colonies (where certain publishers had printed it without Harriet's permission and without paying her any royalty) 1,500,000 copies were sold in the first year.

The book created an enormous stir in England. Although England had outlawed slavery twenty years previously, the living conditions of factory workers there were very poor. Many of these people saw some of their own suffering in the troubles of Uncle Tom. An English antislavery society sent Harriet a scroll signed by 500,000 women, urging her to come to England to speak to its members.

When the invitation arrived, Harriet was in the midst of another move. Calvin was to teach at Andover, Massachusetts, and Harriet went there ahead of him to prepare for her family a house which became known as the Stone Cabin. Also, since so many Southerners had accused Harriet of painting a false picture of slavery, she was preparing an answer to them. It was a book called *The Key to Uncle Tom's Cabin,* which would prove that every incident she had used had actually happened and that every character really existed.

Even in the midst of the hard work of moving and writing, she found time to write Calvin, "It is not fame nor praise that contents me. I seem never to have needed love so much as now. I long to hear you say how much you love me."

As soon as she finished the book and her children were safely in boarding schools or with relatives, Calvin and she sailed for England.

When the ship docked at Liverpool, the Stowes

were astonished to see an enormous crowd waiting to greet the woman who had written *Uncle Tom's Cabin*. Everyplace the train to London stopped, Harriet saw that the people of Britain had taken the book to their hearts. All through the green English countryside people turned out to hail her; in the smoky cities factory workers came to greet and cheer her. A farmer on the Duke of Argyll's estate walked six miles to see her, and Harriet wrote home, "When I put my hand into his great prairie of a palm, I was a grasshopper in my own eyes." At a meeting in Edinburgh, Scotland, she was given 1,000 sovereigns — almost $5,000 — to use for the benefit of slaves; the money had been given in small sums by the people who could least afford it.

It was the same story with people of wealth and importance throughout England and Scotland. It was lucky the book had brought her enough money to buy that silk dress, for she and Calvin met bishops, Cabinet ministers, writers, and members of the aristocracy. At elegant dinners they met such writers as Charles Dickens and William Makepeace Thackeray. All had read her book and were moved by it.

She had cause to remember the long-ago evenings of her childhood when her family read aloud the poems of Lord Byron, for she met and became a friend of the poet's widow. And when she met the pale, fragile poetess Elizabeth Barrett Browning, Mrs. Browning commented, "Never did lioness roar so softly!"

It was enough to turn the most level head — but it didn't turn Harriet's. Just before she had left Andover, someone had written to ask for a description of her, and she had answered, "I am a little bit of a woman, somewhat more than forty, about as thin and dry as a pinch of snuff; never very much to look at in my best days, and looking like a used-up article now."

This was how she still thought of herself that autumn when she and Calvin said good-bye to their English friends and set sail for home.

7. GRIEF COMES

Harriet reached the United States in time to be caught up in the wave of emotion over the debate in Congress about the Kansas-Nebraska Act.

These were years when many of the Midwestern and Western territories were becoming states. Should they allow slavery or not? Up to that time there had been the same number of slave and free states. But now Southern Congressmen were demanding that Kansas and Nebraska be allowed to decide the slavery question for themselves. Slaveowners and rough frontiersmen were poised on the borders, ready to stir up trouble for antislavery settlers there and to make sure proslavery forces won local elections.

Harriet sat down to do what she knew best — write another book. *Dred* would show how slavery caused the corruption of all classes in the South — of slave, slaveowner, and "poor white" farmer — and how the unhappy system ruined even the land. As always, every evening she read her day's work aloud to Calvin and the children, who listened enthralled. They wept, or laughed, or made suggestions, which she followed carefully.

But she interrupted her work to celebrate a very important event — her father's eightieth birthday.

Lyman Beecher had outlived three wives. He was living in Brooklyn then, not far from Henry Ward. He and all his sons and daughters came to the Stone Cabin for the festivities. What a group they were! Lyman still walked everywhere, jumping any wall or fence that stood in his way. He had a habit of taking out his false teeth and forgetting where he left them, but otherwise, he was as alert as ever. When Hattie was brushing his hair before the birthday dinner, she said he was a very handsome old gentleman. Smiling at her mischievously, he said, "Oh, Hattie, tell me something new!"

He had always said of Henry Ward and Hattie that they felt their way with their hearts and followed with their heads. Recently Henry Ward had been making ringing denunciations of the Kansas-Nebraska Act from his pulpit, and his father said, "Thought *I* could preach till I heard Henry!"

Sister Catherine had become domineering. But perhaps she had a right to be. She had founded dozens of schools throughout the frontier territories and staffed them with teachers from New England who needed work. And she had written books on education, health, and housekeeping. Edward Beecher, a vigorous abolitionist, was the

most respected minister in Boston. Harriet's younger half sister Isabella was a leader in the movement to give women the right to vote. Lyman really was, as people said, the father of more brains than any man in the country.

He could look around the birthday table at his children and know that his wish had come true: his seven sons had all become ministers, and three of his four daughters were among the nation's most outstanding women. A small-town preacher could be proud of a family like that!

When Harriet's novel *Dred* reached the bookstores, it sold almost as many copies as *Uncle Tom's Cabin*. To make sure she owned the rights to the book in England, she and Calvin set off across the Atlantic once more, taking the twin girls, Hatty and Eliza, and Henry, the oldest boy.

Harriet's second visit to England was much like her first, except that this time she made the acquaintance of a tiny, very important lady she had not met on her previous visit. Calvin Stowe wrote home about it:

"Yesterday we had just the very pleasantest little interview with the Queen [Victoria] that ever was. None of the formal, drawing-room, breathless receptions, but just an accidental, done-on-purpose meeting at a railway station while on our way to Scotland. The Queen seemed really delighted to see my wife and remarkably glad to see me for her sake."

Queen Victoria could not greet Harriet officially because people of both countries would have taken it as a sign that Great Britain sided with the antislavery forces in America. She would have been accused of meddling in American politics. So the meeting in the railway station had to appear accidental.

Both Calvin and handsome young Henry, now ready for college, had to return home early. So Harriet and the girls went on alone to visit France. Harriet found that French working people were reading a translation of *Uncle Tom's Cabin,* as were many Italians, when she reached Venice and Rome. She learned that the book had been translated into thirty-seven languages.

In late spring of the following year, she returned to Andover — to the greatest heartbreak of her life.

Seventeen-year-old Henry had been a freshman at Dartmouth College, in New Hampshire. One lovely July day, while swimming, he was gripped by a cramp and drowned.

Of all her children, Henry had been the closest to Harriet. When she was "owling about" in one of her absentminded dazes, he was the only one in the family who was patient with her. Friendly and lovable, with fair, curly hair and fine features, he had always made her life happier.

His classmates brought his coffin home to Andover. And Harriet learned, if she had not already known, that no honor on earth could make up for the sight of the dead face she had loved so much.

As soon as the first terrible shock was over, Harriet went to Henry's college in Hanover. There an aged woman, a former slave with five

children still in bondage, called on Harriet to try to comfort her. "You must bear it, for the Lord loves ye," she said. It was a Sunday. And she admitted to Harriet that Sundays were hard for her because she didn't work that day and her thoughts dwelt on her children. Not the ones who had died, she said; they were safe in heaven. "But oh, the other five, I don't know where they are."

In the depths of her own grief Harriet realized that the grief of slave mothers, seeing their children sold away to other masters and lost forever, was terrible because it was preventable. She must go on writing. For that was the only way she could fight to end the terrible evil.

8. WAR APPROACHES

Harriet was disheartened. She wrote her daughter Georgianna that she was "cold, weary . . . dead." The very plants in her room were dying before her eyes, she said, and she hadn't the heart to water them. Everything seemed a burden. "The fact is mama is tired. . . ."

She worked on, however, contributing to a new magazine called the *Atlantic Monthly* and writing two books simultaneously: *The Minister's Wooing* and *The Pearl of Orr's Island.* Meanwhile, *Uncle Tom's Cabin* went on making history. Everyday more Americans read it and became determined to rid the country of slavery.

During the late 1850's it often seemed a losing battle. Just before the Kansas elections, border ruffians swarmed in and took control of the local government. There was bloodshed, turmoil. The antislavery leaders in the Northern states wanted to help their friends in "Bleeding Kansas" defend themselves. Henry Ward Beecher announced from his pulpit that rifles would help far more than Bibles. His followers shipped off to the Kansas settlers crates of rifles marked BIBLES. Thereafter rifles sent to antislavery Kansas settlers were known as Beecher's Bibles.

When Harriet finished her two books, she, Calvin, and all the children except Charley, who was only nine, made a last trip abroad. To this last small Stowe, Calvin wrote a letter telling of their visit to a court of law. They were hustled in through a side entrance and suddenly found themselves among wigged and robed judges. "It was enough to frighten a body into fits, but we took it quietly as we could, and your mamma looked as meek as Moses in her little, battered straw hat and gray cloak, seeming to say, 'I didn't come her o' purpose.' "

Later, he wrote, they visited the Duchess of Sutherland. "The great, noble, brilliant duchess came sailing down the stairs to meet us in her white morning dress....Took your mamma into her great bosom and folded her up till the little Yankee woman looked like a small gray kitten half covered in a snowbank...."

They were traveling through Italy that winter when word reached them of a dramatic and frightening event that had just taken place in the United States. An abolitionist named John Brown led a group of men in a raid on a government arsenal in Harpers Ferry, Virginia. His plan was to use the arms to free slaves. But Brown and his surviving followers were taken prisoner by Colonel Robert E. Lee. And six weeks later Brown was hanged for treason.

It was hard for Harriet to be away from her country at such a time. But she needed a rest; she still had not recovered from Henry's death. She tried to keep herself occupied, looking at Roman ruins, olive groves, and rocky cliffs reaching down to the blue Mediterranean. But constantly the memory of Henry's face rose before her eyes.

She started another story, *Agnes of Sorrento.* However, even work could not keep her thoughts from her lost son. Long before it was time to return, she was desperately homesick.

In the United States, the new Republican Party held a convention to decide on whom to nominate for President. They wanted a candidate who was against extending slavery into any more states, but who was not an abolitionist. A mild and reasonable man, they thought, would be more acceptable to the Southern and border states. So they chose a tall, thin, homely Illinois lawyer, Abraham Lincoln.

Harriet, when she arrived home, was disappointed at the choice because she was afraid he would not really try to free the slaves. She supported him halfheartedly, as did her family.

The South was not to be placated. When Lincoln won the election in November, South

Carolina angrily seceded from the Union. Ten other Southern states followed. They did what John Brown had been hanged for doing: They seized United States' arsenals.

Then South Carolina guns fired on Fort Sumter, and fighting started in earnest. When President Lincoln called for volunteers to put down the Southern rebellion, young men who had read *Uncle Tom's Cabin* flocked to enlist. One of the first was a medical student from Harvard College — Frederick Stowe.

He came home in a rumpled, outsized Army uniform to tell his parents that he had joined up. Harriet's heart sank. In the last dozen years she had lost one baby son, one son almost grown. How could she bear it if anything happened to Freddie?

She begged him to finish his medical studies first. But Freddie answered that he could never face his fellowmen. "People shall never say Harriet Beecher Stowe's son is a coward!"

9. HARRIET MEETS MR. LINCOLN

The speech Lincoln made when he was sworn into office in April, 1861, seemed to be a plea to the South for peace. It was not his intention, he said, to interfere with slavery where it already existed. But secession could not be allowed. Later, to Harriet's indignation, he would say, "My paramount object in this struggle is to save the Union, and it is not either to save or destroy slavery. If I could save the Union without freeing any slave, I would do it. . . ."

Not so Harriet. To her, the Union itself was less important than the liberty of the slaves.

Freddie had joined the Army to fight her battle; her book had made him enlist. It was a heavy responsibility. When his company arrived in New Jersey, she hurried there to see him.

He caught sight of her and came rushing toward her, "bristling with knapsack, and haversack, and looking like an assortment of packages," she wrote Calvin. How hot and dusty he looked! Her first thought was to wipe his face with her handkerchief before she kissed him — as she had done so often when he was a little boy.

At the same camp she saw her brother Charles' son. And he, like Freddie, looked suddenly grown-up. "So our boys come to manhood in a day," she wrote.

Freddie was in the first great Battle of Bull Run but didn't get a chance to fire his gun — except once at a pig, which his squad roasted and ate. The battle itself went against the Union Army, and the Northerners began to realize that it would not be a quick victory. Things might get worse — and they did.

Harriet felt there was a kind of terrible justice in the Union losses, because for so many years the North had consented to slavery in the South — conspired in it, profited by it, and looked the other way. She felt that in the eyes of God, both North and South were equally guilty.

The whole first year of the war and part of the second, it was one loss after another for the Union troops.

In November Harriet went to Washington to a Thanksgiving dinner held for several thousand former slaves — now fugitive or freed. She heard a sermon of thanksgiving by a blind old Negro and listened to thousands of voices singing a spiritual:

> Tell King Pharaoh
> To let my people go!

Lincoln was still being cautious about freedom for the slaves. Harriet went to the White House to try to learn what he intended to do.

When she was ushered in, Lincoln was sitting in front of a coal fire warming his hands. He unfolded his long body and came across the room to shake hands. "So this is the little woman who wrote the book that made this big war!" he said.

Then he led her to the fireside, and they sat down. "I do like an open fire," he said. "I always had one to home." He told her he had not declared for abolition sooner because he had not wanted to anger the border states, where feelings about slavery were mixed. But now their sentiment was with the Union, and he felt he could take the step. In three months, he said, unless the South asked for peace first, his Emancipation Proclamation would become law. All slaves in the rebellious states would be declared free.

At last Harriet could support this wise, homely man wholeheartedly.

On New Year's Day, 1863, she went to a concert in Boston. She was sitting in the gallery when a man came on stage and announced that President Lincoln had signed the Emancipation Proclamation. The audience yelled and cheered. Then someone discovered Harriet, and everyone waved to her and insisted that she stand. A little flustered, she rose, bowed, smiled. Then the whole audience stood up and cheered the woman whose book had contributed so much toward this day.

10. VICTORY AND SADNESS

In January, 1863, when old Lyman Beecher died, it was a time of trial for the Union Army. Still suffering from losses at Fredericksburg, the Army lost again at Chancellorsville. Even when it won ground, losses in men were heavy. Hospitals were filled to overflowing. Many women of the North volunteered as nurses, or rolled bandages, knit socks, and made blankets. Harriet's weapon, as always, was her pen.

She was deeply troubled by a grave threat to the Union. Many of England's leaders were siding with the Southern states. Powerful merchants and owners of British factories, who looked on America's Northern industries as dangerous competitors, needed the South's cotton to keep their mills running. Since the South had no navy, owners of British shipyards were happy to build ships for the Confederacy. Business in British shipyards was booming. Many members of Parliament wanted the British government to recognize the Confederacy officially.

Harriet wrote a strong letter to the women of England, urging them to support the Union's fight against slavery. She heard that her letter had "covered some with shame, and it has compelled many to think, and it has stimulated not a few to act."

Meanwhile, Henry Ward was speaking for the North in the industrial centers of England and Scotland. He told miners and factory workers that the Union was fighting for the freedom and the rights of working people all over the world. Thousands came to hear him. Many who came to shout him down stayed to cheer. Before he

returned home, British sympathy for the North had become so strong that there was no more talk in Parliament of recognizing the Confederacy.

Later Harriet heard that the South's General Robert E. Lee said Britain and France would have recognized the Confederacy if it had not been for Henry Ward Beecher's speeches and Harriet's *Uncle Tom's Cabin.*

In July, 1863, the people of the North heard that their forces had won a great victory at Gettysburg, Pennsylvania. But the price in lives had been costly. After the battle, Charles Beecher received word that his oldest son had been wounded, possibly fatally. And at the Stone Cabin in Andover, Harriet and Calvin Stowe received a similar letter. Captain Frederick Stowe — their Freddie — was badly wounded.

Freddie recovered. But a piece of shell had pierced his ear and entered his brain, and he never was quite the same again.

The winter of 1864–1865 was the last winter of the war — the end of the weary, uphill climb to victory. When Harriet went to Washington to pay another visit to President Lincoln, she found him tired and worn beyond belief. Didn't he feel better, she asked, now that it seemed the war might end?

Lincoln smiled wearily and said, "Mrs. Stowe, I shall never live to see peace. This war is killing me."

In March, as fresh spring grass covered old battlefields, the Confederate armies fought their last battles and were defeated. When Union troops recaptured Fort Sumter and the American flag was raised over it, Henry Ward Beecher delivered a sermon of thanksgiving. As Lincoln said, "Without Beecher in England, there might not have been a flag to raise."

At last, early in April, Lee surrendered the remnants of his army at Appomattox, Virginia. The war was over. But one mad act remained.

Five days after Lee's surrender, President Lincoln was assassinated.

And Harriet wrote, "The kind, hard hand that

held the helm so steadily in the desperate toss-
ings of the storm, has been stricken down just
as we entered port....The eyes are yet too dim
with tears that would seek calmly to rate our
Abraham Lincoln's place in history...."

11. THE QUIET YEARS

When Hattie was a schoolgirl in Hartford, she had found a grove of oaks near a little river where she wanted to build a house if she ever became a famous writer and could afford it. Just before the end of the war, she returned to Hartford and bought the land. Most of the money she had earned from her many books poured into building a house there. She called it Oakholm. She and Calvin loved it, and Freddie regained some of his strength there.

Within a few years, still trying to restore Freddie to health, the Stowes bought an orange grove at Mandarin Cove, Florida. There, in peace and seclusion, they would spend their winters and live summers in Hartford.

Harriet continued to write. Her *Oldtown Folks* was a collection of stories of Calvin's youth in Natick, Massachusetts. Ten years later she wrote about her childhood in a book called *Poganuc People.* Her best writings, though not her most popular, were stories of New England life.

The twins, Eliza and Hatty, never married but spent their lives running the household, working as Harriet's secretaries, and trying to keep their two absentminded parents from blundering into complete chaos. Tomboy Georgianna May married — a minister, naturally — and gave Harriet her first grandchild. "Our Charley," whose exploits as a child had kept readers of the *Atlantic Monthly* entertained, went to sea

several times during his teens, then came home, and settled down to become a minister.

Freddie, after trying hopelessly to make something of himself, left home. He was determined not to return until his nerves and willpower were restored. He disappeared in San Francisco and was never heard from again. For years Harriet lived in the vain hope that he would come back home.

Calvin passed his old age happily surrounded by his books. He had spent much of his life writing a history of the Bible. Finally, in 1880, Harriet managed to get the pages away from him and off to a publisher. To Calvin's astonishment the book brought him $10,000 in royalties.

Harriet's declining years were tranquil. Famous and beloved Americans like James Russell Lowell, John Greenleaf Whittier, and Henry Wadsworth Longfellow were her friends and admirers. Her neighbors loved her, and her family remained close to her. She took tender care of Calvin until his death.

At last, in the early 1890's, she wrote a friend, "My sun has set. The time of work for me is over. I have written all my words and thought all my thoughts, and now I rest me in the flickering light of the dying embers." She deserved a rest. She had written twenty-three books, countless short stories, essays, magazine articles, even hymns. And one of her books had awakened the conscience of the world.

The first night of July, 1896, she woke from a coma, saying, "Oh, I have had such a beautiful dream!" She looked at the nurse who had taken faithful care of her during the last weeks and said, "I love you." Then she died.

INDEX

The Author

JEAN ROUVEROL, the widow of screenwriter Hugo Butler, has written motion pictures and a great variety of fiction. At the age of seventeen she had the lead in a Broadway play written by her mother and later acted in motion pictures and radio dramas. The mother of six children, she has found that one of her greatest pleasures is reading aloud to young people. Her home is in Los Angeles.